T0154297

PHRASIS

WENDY XU

PHRASIS

The Ottoline Prize
Selected by HOA NGUYEN

FENCE BOOKS
ALBANY, NY

Cover design by Fence Books
Interior by Jess Puglisi

Published in the United States by Fence Books

Science Library, 320
University at Albany
1400 Washington Avenue
Albany, NY 12222

FENCEPORTAL.ORG

This book was printed by TK and distributed by Small Press
Distribution (spdbooks.org) and Consortium Book Sales and
Distribution (cbsd.com).

Library of Congress Cataloguing in Publication Data
Xu, Wendy [1987–]
Phrasis / Wendy Xu

Library of Congress Control Number: 2017930667

ISBN 13: 978-1-934200-94-0

FIRST EDITION
10 9 8 7 6 5 4 3 2

PHRASIS

·

·

The eye is the first circle; the horizon which
it forms is the second; and throughout nature
this primary figure is repeated without end

RALPH WALDO EMERSON

.

No circles / but that two parallels do cross

JOHN WIENERS, *A POEM FOR PAINTERS*

The silver sheen of water, children marking it with fists
Industrious lights along the historic bridge
I am touched by a flower vendor bending to
    a child and record it to you, here
Wind in the irons for a moment, almost soft
The poem vandalizing my original face, so let it work
    ever against my body

Recovery

Whatever the vectors pushed off into, a flight
inching home in snow, you in your delighted
heavy abstraction. I was an egg and more eggs swimming
in the margin's pool. Life is vague and vaguer when
we still kneeling in front of the television push
a finger inside. I smoke alone in my room, the war was
a disambiguation across platforms, notably its own
eddying to music. The it of love was on my mind.

A halo of newsprint, when I became alone I claimed
the greedy living text, jasmine, the sink sang
its steam about the house. The war was a syntactical
construction pointing back toward itself when I
could not turn off the radio's list of fatalities. I locked
my literal body inside the green deadbolt. The house breathed
its hotter mouth, when I became alone the whiter hand
of my country sweeping toward me.

Phrasis

Stilled as in image, at dawn sliding into
blue harbor, boats clang, where does he
the man I imagine gripping several ropes
return from. Is he conflicted, does he
perceive the sky oscillating like
a dimmer machine, a mouth, a war, language
not declaring its most
effective self. *Bellum* grazing ever nearer
to beauty, a possible apotheosis how
what is left of sense
is comfort. Not inebriated much anymore
I rented a lawn to stand in, crueler
was always signing to our mutual forks,
knives. Our translation
of a subject drones
on unblinking, something black for him
returning, his forearms there laid
themselves down, ships gone out another
pale-plated night.

Winter Missive

What anyone intended a life to be
arriving at the dim shore and stacked
many deep, saying to loved ones I feel
unnatural, half a human face smothered
in deep light. How preciously next
our leaders beating the thin song out
from in us. I chinned up when each
trembling kind of weather
was mine, the hills stood heavy
all white. To clouds I am too little
a message, say O cloud go
to cities cut out from others, go down
and lay your soft
to decent soft, be there when we looking up
and through you. When of
that sudden mirror, that sky ledge, clear
not ever blue.

Some People

I had a theory, it flung its scent over
every shadow surface. One human apartment, one
comes to a loud boil in the morning. If they found
me oblique then I am doing this for my bluer
augmented self now. Fear of the unannounced
colloquial war, or, I liked it when the sullen man said
just leave your name. The restaurant
was crowded. The news was deathwatches
are available, I felt devoted to my new angel
of losing time. Categorical elegy. Something I thought
today was system error, was reverent, was one
or orbiting nothing. No other.

The Window Rehearses

There in the window it was speaking
to an expanse and wider
sense, noxious, nightly perfume
trails sidelong then
more away. I did doubt the little
sparer house its rooms
opened to dark, to further thought we first
saw the grove there, as is it
just is, was imminent despairing spent
over breakfast. There in double
window panes it hung
its fruit, airing
bitterly its juice, its chiming
to us a history. Swaying to we
preposterous two
against silence a cracking of hands
there in windows
framed us. I perform well
my surface for you.
He there of the slight, bent frame
conducts a symphony, lies
down upon a year's heat
still waving. There in the window it
remembers a chaos
lacking snow, what will excuse

our sleep then, the balcony, driving both
hands into the space I
am allowed. Not broadly gaming
a day and there, in the bend
of a window see it becoming some
late other self.

Disclosure for Solo Violin

Dragged through and away from hands, the long years

At the mirror chewed up but spit not once in the faces
of others

Once, the self hung out its rough shell, radially dark

Some nights it gasped the tyrannical little song and
was so pleased

I emerged grinning and unformed, loving you well enough

Ocean to pink ruddy shore

Moved through a day famishing, no sleep 'til Brooklyn
rightly

We built it then

Nests growing enormous and trails behind, your color

Not red

．

A breath here, how to reprimand the surface of it
Drifting to sleep in my contact lenses I begin to despair
We did everything humanely possible
"Characterized by tenderness, not a reproach of, an act of"
The television, our daily panic chorus
"I accomplish, therefore I am"

By Action

Thinking to see them there, captains
industrious in
morning sun, I crack the egg's tender
yellow head

Love comes to me un-
repentant, toward it all vectors
converge repeating, like

moment of the necessary form
I pluck a feather from your neck

On the page one alights without permission, or
love is
an assemblage

beginning each day identical, palpable I
remarks of, is it that music or need edits
my body

two people leave a shopping mall
with goods, death squad hovering high
a streetlamp
Call your mother, stay up late

to watch the neighborhood

undressing light, like
multiple phone calls
connected then
hung up, get the family together soon, watch

American bison overtake the field
filling a vehicle lane in early snow
obstructed I paused
To see it, their dark furs shaking enormous
out of trees they descended from the line of sky
respond to a much deeper instinct

we were then back on our way
input later to the search bar
I love keywords, like
love is
an exodus

I imagine you sleeping, then a pyramid or
chandelier throwing sunlight

An absence emerges, sharp
I regard the whole
practice of it

touch it

Diagonal Sun

I wanted so bad all that rustic shit
his multinational super-sound of distressed
love, his parting public

vocal lament
The dresser arrives to us as promised
was like summer lo-fi altruism, believing
before my good looks time out

I'll write beneath my own name
on principle
At the beach prodding another hoax
they cradled her mermaid head

through the double white doors, a face
you would kiss that sexy
purple tail like Hey, *lighten up*
She'll look at you when you talk to her given

the choice of paranoias I turn down
premium love
its concerned porcelain corners, consume

more fantasy than I produce

when all men save mine
are dead, others still sow the wild
green potato for pay, does he push upon you

a needlework formalism though
The dream of the grid bent over
there in the sun

Task Force

Moved all the way here to watch
television alone, swallowed by the grim

news grinning. Fuck a five year plan, first
one passes through Tiananmen the gate

of heavenly peace, emptied public square finery
in summer, purple cupping red azaleas

Happy birth upon a time, Nation!
Reveling in my love for him coquettish

worried, approaching paranoia
for the home country removed that June

The cropped photo best dilated
in our pockets black and white

It was a long hard road continuously reading
analysis metrics, my father knew a guy

worked in sales, was there and saw
them roll in like nothing else

Black pillars to the effective dispersal

I felt nothing pulling
from the airport's narrowing gate
In the photo we still get perfectly centered

Longview the idiot's
consumption guide, naturally then

my love for was only

Sunday

It takes a tree's patience, illuminating all
that year I was drunk babbling
of the low sounding brook, black rock cliffs
just falling away from the postcard's
catchy corner
I got right with myself, you know?
The disaster abroad had so much money
in the bank, popularized dissent spreading

warm red, remove yourself
from the screen if you can, maybe
When I wake up I don't
even know what I'm not
still looking for, you hanging ugly

those purple heart-shaped leaves
In a single phrase I'd call it "Damn
Good Drama"
Ad hoc for the particularly pretty requiem
Paychecks arriving Friday, no sooner we flutter

to the corporate prom, but
did we touch
anything there deeper, some depth say
"the human spirit" called

to explain upon one's self, five hits
of the pillow without you
takes to task and beyond

I set out early and bright wanting nothing
You get nothing
Nobody can judge you, nobody shall

Civil Dusk

As an object does, perhaps turning
in place, fixed orbit satisfies
my aesthetic need

Off-stage a roaring fire
Shafts of light gesture in separate directions

between the hole where
I emerge and where I never get
any sleep, just a few feet

Night stopped softly by I worried
over seeming clever or
unfeeling, rather

like damaged roses
Their scent trailing a hot factory, not
Taiwan or Manila where the news anchor

loathes her boss
When the news anchor
quits her job some of us
got loaded, hopped up on rooftops

lewd views
made a reality of
getting into art early for whom?
Solar noon
approximate equation for the poem's
degraded center like

I'm once again stuck
in the cross streets without
a bathroom
mapping app

Grace under fair weather, brevity

under God
under pressure

Arrangements

At one end signal any cloud, early-ish,
    looking around

I half desire particulars of a walnut

The dream of who I do not kill comes to me eager

Linen shirts crisping out a line, I having dressed two

I come apart, clean white shifting
    from happier notes

Boxes still lean the dignified window

The dream of the dignified window

Naturalism

Wind lifts strangely in lines
of dissent, like care, all men blur together becoming
a great nothing. I say to a friend *all men*
are worse. No time for anchor design
in a relative statement, one must fling aside
    sheepishness though

I want my face to be blown on, an ideal
unachievable through practice or
"visual art." I was there on the green bridge nightly

watched eels swim dark a river's curvature
their forms twisted among rocks,
we were holding on
to the day's trash and cigarettes in one
shared pocket. I wash the dishes

even here, slowing, I can again regard your sentences
in public. This thought that lodges: venture capitalists
of America, kill yourselves

out in the blueberry barrens red
and purple mountains
and situating a view of wilderness upending sky
our inefficacy complaining, say *nature*
is amazing, the sentences in spades and nowhere
to keep them, quietly we sat down

to watch the land, nothing made
of us a roaming target
It was not evaluative then nor
is it now
our love
did not wear its body outside to die in the cooler months
Nothing was a weapon when I drink
my coffee after the dog, fat plums beneath my heel
Here is outside the structure pertaining sympathy

So sensitive
subject positioning, I felt at odds and had
my elbow licked
To speak on intention it was mnemonic, bright star
was a calling back subtle
the image: almost asleep
blue phone ringing in the dark

．

The word derives from our habit of naming empty
    space, our mark there

A catalogue then, of the present as it shifts into rose view

Phrasis

Imagine a person upon whom nothing is lost,
pulling the purple cabbages up head by head, half
like devotional

Those welts blossom your skin plural, you looking
at me like nothing I need

I put down the mildest impressions of light, strict
bodied, giving you uninvaded space and how divided?

Referring to the self in thirds, he there of the bent
frame, she shaded in multiplicities of orange, red

I say to another *fuck yeah* kind of night, burning
the candle at both intonations of a flame

I say to nobody about the inner life, moon so
recently super, then gone, then equivalent reducing
you again to yourself

Sub par, rolling the smokeless tube between my big
teeth I feel repeatedly scandalized, I touch
your bad knees

Preemptive necessity is a phrase I'd like to unframe,
people do plunder each other, teethed, telling you
what you are

When they brought us the ottoman I called to you
from the shower, thought I did, didn't I, I did

Thought I would learn the older ways, how a space
figurally extends otherwise bleak horizons

Impressed another's man this morning in vivid ochre,
one's vocabulary lies down brightly, thinks better of

Watching you watch the news turning, gently overture
of coal streaks dark onto dark, a bee on a bud

A root's bitterness is edged out, sweetened the pot, I
am telling you I speak from the representative *we* but
do not fill me in

Women did not say *color is its own autonomous expression
of feeling* not bounded to the object, the expression of
the object

The colored figure is four and each added slowly,
according, to each further color, blues into
further rooms

Not wanting to procedure the flesh and blood
morning, one leaves behind its fantasy, softening

All color is gratuitous smeared against the grain, red
fang glowing just hangs there, shakes a gaunt leaf off

After breaking particularly long period of hermitage,
you reek again of industry

I could watch you dream big from your station in
life, mutually silence holds our friends together
in this trying, these times

In upper and lower variance my attitude was polite,
in two days sounds the house again of you

———

They pressed you to dredge unused methods,
an integer of color ennobles them against you,
luminist, suddenly the light

Concealing methods, does my intention sink or strike

Scene fades to black. You move to the machine,
plumbed, beyond which my grammar correctly
cannot follow

How a woman says do not only paint me as your
public pleases

How I expressed love stirring the beans, a cough
swells white space proportional to its source

My source text was unresponsive and so varying
methods, slashed it pink instead

Maudlin, from Mary, the first word in lying on a
couch to be alone with you, crying up no
night's sleep

I read a book where one speaks for another beneath
a balcony, some of wording love is for the idea of soul

A woman is married to the campground
where she reflects upon the whole of her life,
where she embraces the feeling of song

A gentleman paints the inner life and plunges
hands repeatedly into the violence of history, meets
˙ nobody in the abstract middle

Moved far past sense, the aperture shuttering your
image though I accept dying plunged in a vat
of light, or is it yellow

I make my needs on a page, the black pool dries
shapely, a needle, a hawk, tougher when your pot
roils over

What if truly one builds an empire of doubt, waters
it and thus sensationally, blasts into newer years, a year

Your sentence riddles me darkly, flows hard, a mist
of blue inks pushed across the wider canvas

———

I having been so sentimental, modernity, still
alive, usually saying *this* or *that* toward everything
in particular

I lived with you then inside a colloquial century,
hardly possible to be still adjourned into
brighter meaning

The Forecast

Distrust this season breeds
in me whole
blue worlds, am second
to leafy nouns
pinned back darkening lip
of the night,
untrustworthy sidewalk glazed
and sleeping there,
peachy trees, a line drawn from one
brow of a star down
and planted, each pillow
little shimmer, little wilt startled
from out the arranging field
moonlit pale behind
no foxes, in me finding the fragrant
new crisis, not dead still
where I love you in feast
and pledge, worlds rolling first
on crookedly
and on.

Poem For Fathers

FOR FRANK LIMA

First fathers lie down, unmake
the world in any

old image, a deep black cup,
your hairbrush, the shape

of a whetstone ground
thin and away. Good enough pieced

from the blur a body runs
to the end of its pillars,

they gifted us the ragged
affectionate tape and we spooled the earth

in half, surely a face formed there
purely by will.

This Quiet

The cactus blooms itself
in air, is going places, is not
and never has been a vision
of anyone's hand
laboring nightly. I give
to others and in keeping
none, am ferried, visibly away
from faces in the light.
If I bridge well
some chasm, make my effort
with people then
does anyone become a companion
still waking, still gone or low
snarling in a dream, up
now for discussion of how
a word goes on regarding
its shadow. We had all manner
of speaking not in bodies
splayed likewise lurch
and stutter. But tenderly
a finger set
to music.

The Years

Such were they, a dumb stuffed thing
to say, if truth is we all grow old un-

observed, limbs flail only halfway up
a flight, where does dark begin settling

my little bones. I dream and do love
to have them, blue fish

in a lake, my head more tipped up than down
under damp earth. Some days others like deer

from the shot, peeled back, how I
find trees dressed in wild

green light. The years come, unstitched
a face, saddled as one would a heavy beast

for walking. Likely I became then a member
of heaven, put up, the years come and reaching

their long wet hands.

Theme Song

Unrested we said to others leave
us pleased, not far along our track, still much

we want, half the slower good death
of cities too off your bristling map.

People demand two and then more hours
in a room already settled. Reverently I

am a kind of pulled down, mucking poorly
the clean slate, it was only how we

say tragic, notes shoved off
into blue air. In the morning asking others

how not to die and bury, when is a resting all
together now to music. Set upon a high place once

and am ruined, what is after drawn
sweetly by love, doors fixed

to a theme, likely then we wash ourselves
against one another.

．

Of a mandatory binding agent native to your practice

Ding a rod to strike perfect tension, body opulent

Everyone done up in cream oils

When time remains to show him my love, cynical,
    sweating through the suburbs

Azure and tar, still

I lick the greening verb to rest

Five Year Plan

No great thoughts today relaxing
behind the factory loft
I scrawled cornflower

in the margins, ethical verbs
The image removed as to finally
be regarded I consider
the view: shiny green flies

displaced hibiscus
in the adjoining dark

On the train I worry a stranger's
jutted hip and miss
that country view, bionic
or landscape
optimal verve reaches someone

in partial address
Out all day I wish more bars
and restaurants unto nobody
Crystalline rain on a bird's

soft foot, the line was unsteady strung up
between wet buildings
What I saw framed beyond the window
reduced in quality
there sharpening

October Sift

In one story God speaks to the weary sailor
on existence as uninspired fact, shoves off the brittle
white boat toward steaming
distant mountains
Unlikely that consciousness remained there
within him, peak conditions for song if we
        propose fatigue
coloring in its own note but it
was October and the data stream was calling
out like I do finally blue
gently bluer, soft even imagining
the spectral dictum yawning itself beside me

When I lived in the country I built no monuments,
took it as my job assembling
the obvious field
A crown of seagulls, glass sea, from it removing
now my disappointment over kids arrested
on the train for what? Trading indeed
in likenesses the ugly work I laid
my cheek down upon the mattress, how to do
the next part
bristling undone

E-Spiritual

Electrical box fizzling out rapid, here at the beach
the stairs bore our weight down and beneath
both stories
Flash phone light lit off
In the description of your trip visiting someone's
    generous mother

what is spiritual or particular in the bite-sized
undigestable retelling? It goes "moved optimistically
to the country," checking per-head prices
    for the milk-goat's young online
Rise and trying to shine though
The seven bordering ranges looking down our valley

harbor a disconnect whereby how are we
to make a living?
My students, bless them, all white up here

clapping the ancient chalk
A despair over vocation if like you, I too
am on the platform
looking across

Past irony in the moment everyone's a goddamm peach
that green tweed, Sir, your authority's showing again

I humble bragged the office manager after work
in and out of service I said "but baby," thought
    my sweet love calling
me home, and anxious, devastated
by the newly outfitted pipeline news
buried there ugly overnight
It remains though that bellied up to the bar's wet corner

I was unaccounted for, concerned citizens
    worrying away
the urban beach's future beneath

the neon palms, kissing him late
and flickers
and bears no further fruit

Micro Portrait

En masse we assembled here for the naming
    of tragic rooms

It was too quiet, called back toward you in monochrome

The weather was all salt dragging across the hardwood

I alone approach the image, it does not disappoint,
    bleeds across my tapes

Blue was its sole intention revising your earlier dictation

If one looks hard and finding you good for nothing

Am I so wilted I trail a heavy foot across the line,
    there is evidence you stay alive

If I look back and cleanly pause

Next do not look again

Music Box

I tried on the house, its shutters dressed white

See it there wasting behind trees, the light and with it

Our looking into a field beyond four corners of a frame

Music begins in the body, moves out

I appear myself in public brimming nearer
    the bronze fountain

People gather up their people, half in-scene

Placed by principles of natural order I open
    my mouth

My language slips through and through me again

Work

Last night I slogged hours into the paperwork
and stayed there, heavier still into speech dragging
my body too
The architecture was cleaving along

supernatural lines, this week's weather
defeating the next like a post-popular
tropical event even cuter
than last year's devastating landfall
You deserve a one-act play of irreverence
    commemorating

wealthy neighbors who buy up all the art
eating sweetened granola outside the window I wish
your epistolary garden view like

when you say Auden I hear rare silver birds
    mistaking
the naturalist for the poet, isn't shit just funny that way
Shutter-shock canary yellow in the wide

middling field, or is it nearer
the industrial lot beneath my window where men
shovel up the last

of summer's good black dirt, I was still all alone
    in the park
staring up at the Egyptian obelisk's worn
southern face while joggers touched me now
and then by accident
You ran with them for a moment beneath
    the bright canopy
I joined several witnesses calling softly back
you by your name

Phrasis

Invited to bring ourselves to a winter, America filling
　　with gun-metal, grey

I lived with you inside a devotional view

The church there behind whiter ridges sang to us

Hardened as if through the television's red accumulation

First the eyes, though I had no feeling for description

Made alive through a century not brought before
　　the senses

The flight carrying on, unmanned, the dishwasher
　　stands before dishes

Slips a warm hand into

You come home after a job, lie down beneath
    no mountains

Not lagging of body nor spirit

From my station I am given the news, open-palmed
    it comes to me ripening

Bowed and salty we now admiring the lengthwise sky

Snow proposes slowly to us an order

What did I learn then, nightly clutched the stars
    and song

Tuning the dial to hear unknown personage

If we remember its happening

The echo carried out starving from the body

Is it then infinitely occurring

Does it then incur the news back toward us

Speak of it, against inarticulable black objects circling

I was barely how a city calls to you prospective,
   the highway

Driving toward what I imagine now was a water tower

Our friends soon unknowing one and then another

If a man returns home doubling his debts, dreams
   courage for a wife

The news found us chewing our rich fat

The longer table where I inside my gold
   performed a year

The dishwasher sees it there, plunges scraps
   of the avocado into water

We strung out heavier notes ironing the field

Called out to us, our innumerable names

I had lived with you vivid inside a century's noise,
   music turned over within me

A little house, in the window there we saw it first
    shining safe and away

Here it is again smearing its light to bluer, your light

Acknowledgments

Grateful acknowledgment is given to the following journals, where many of these poems first appeared, often in slightly different forms:

Bat City Review, "Micro Portrait"
Brooklyn Magazine, "Poem for Fathers"
Denver Quarterly, "This Quiet"
Everyday Genius, "Music Box"
Guernica, "The Years"
Hyperallergic, "By Action"
jubilat, "Recovery," "Some People"
Narrative Magazine, "Winter Missive"
PEN Poetry Series, "The Window Rehearses,"
    "Theme Song"
Poetry, "The Forecast," "Phrasis (Stilled)"

The poems "Music Box," "Sunday," "Task Force," "Theme Song," "Naturalism," "Phrasis (Invited)" and "Phrasis (Imagine)" were collected in an audio-chapbook from Black Cake Records.

Several poems were published in a chapbook in 2015 from Brooklyn Arts Press, entitled Naturalism.

Thank you to my teachers and advocates, for hearing me then and now, and for their kind words: James Tate, Peter Gizzi, Dara Wier, D.A. Powell, James Haug, Solmaz Sharif, David Tomas Martinez, and Tan Lin.

My deepest thanks to the Poetry Foundation and the Program for Poets & Writers at UMass-Amherst for giving me time, encouragement, and resources, without which this book would not exist.

Thank you to Hoa Nguyen for choosing this book, and Rebecca Wolff, Paul Legault, and Jess Puglisi for realizing it.

Thank you to every friend who ever read a draft of a poem, every classmate who ever made time for my work — thank you for making my life possible.

Thank you to Jess Grover, to whom this book owes a tremendous debt.

To my parents, Deping and Ning, and my sister Cindy, for their courage and fierce love.

Thank you to Jonathan Larson, for everything: big, small, daily, immeasurable.

Born in Shandong, China, in 1987, Wendy Xu is
the author of *You Are Not Dead* (Cleveland State
University Poetry Center, 2013), and the chapbook
Naturalism (Brooklyn Arts Press, 2015). Her poems
have appeared in *The Best American Poetry, Boston Review,
Poetry, A Public Space*, and elsewhere. She was awarded
the Patricia Goedicke Prize in Poetry in 2011,
and a Ruth Lilly and Dorothy Sargent Rosenberg
Fellowship from the Poetry Foundation in 2014.
She lives and teaches writing in New York City.

The Ottoline Prize—named for Lady Ottoline Violet Anne Morrell (1873-1938), beloved undersung patron of the Bloomsbury Group—awards publication and a cash prize to a book of poems by a woman writing in English who has previously published one or more books of poetry. The Ottoline Prize was incarnated previously as the Motherwell Prize, and as the Alberta Prize before that.

The Ottoline Prize

Phrasis	Wendy Xu
Journal of Ugly Sites & Other Journals	Stacy Szymaszek
Inter Arma	Lauren Shufran

The Motherwell and Alberta Prizes

Negro League Baseball	Harmony Holiday
living must bury	Josie Sigler
Aim Straight at the Fountain and Press Vaporize	Elizabeth Marie Young
Unspoiled Air	Kaisa Ullsvik Miller
The Cow	Ariana Reines
Practice, Restraint	Laura Sims
A Magic Book	Sasha Steensen
Sky Girl	Rosemary Griggs
The Real Moon of Poetry and Other Poems	Tina Brown Celona
Zirconia	Chelsey Minnis

FB